Aquascaping:
Aquarium Landscaping
Like a Pro
Second Edition

Aquarist's Guide to Planted
Tank Aesthetics and Design

Artistic Aquascaping styles, live aquarium plants and decorations, substrate, rocks, coral, reefs, lightening, setup, and maintenance

By Moe Martin

Aquascaping: Landscaping Like a Pro
Aquarist's Guide to Planted Tank Aesthetics and Design
Second Edition

Artistic Aquascaping styles, live aquarium plants and decorations, substrate, rocks, coral reefs, lightening, setup, and maintenance

Author: Moe Martin

Copyright © 2013 by: Ubiquitous Publishing

ubiquitouspublishing.com

ISBN: 978-1-927870-10-5

Dedication

This book is dedicated to my mother who was always trying to get me to try new things and develop my interests. I am very happy to have the support of a loving partner as well, who encouraged me to put all my thoughts on aquascaping in a central resource for people with the same passions as me to enjoy and hopefully learn from. Lastly, I would like to thank Takashi Amano for raising the bar in aquascaping to a whole new level. Without all these people, this book would not have been written.

Disclaimer

This book is designed to provide information on aquascaping only. This information is provided and sold with the knowledge that the publisher and author do not offer any legal or other professional advice. In the case of a need for any such expertise consult with the appropriate professional. This book does not contain all information available on the subject. This book has not been created to be specific to any individual's or organizations' situation or needs. Every effort has been made to make this book as accurate as possible. However, there may be typographical and or content errors. Therefore, this book should serve only as a general guide and not as the ultimate source of subject information. This book contains information that might be dated and is intended only to educate and entertain. The author and publisher shall have no liability or responsibility to any person or entity regarding any loss or damage incurred, or alleged to have incurred, directly or indirectly, by the information contained in this book. You hereby agree to be bound by this disclaimer or you may return this book within the guarantee time period for a full refund.

Acknowledgements

I would like to thank my two children for inspiring me to write this book. This has been a hobby of mine for quite some time, and I felt there was a shortage of information out there on aquascaping in one central area - so I took the liberty to create a book about it. There are a lot of details that must be followed for success while maintaining an artistic sense of beauty - all the way from planting to choosing the life that will live in it. My late father was always teaching me the importance of passing on knowledge to others, and so with this book, I honor his memory.

I'd also like to extend my thanks to my spouse who wasn't crazy about the idea of dedicating a room in our home to aquascaping, but now the whole family - including the cats - are more intrigued. They now realize how cool it really is and want to participate in my projects. I'm very grateful for all their love and support.

Lastly, there are so many people in the online community that I admire and respect within this hobby. I would like to thank them as a whole for their contributions - always willing to share one or many of their ideas and inspire others.

There is much to be learned about Aquascaping, and this book contains it all!

Table of Contents

Foreword

Aquascaping is a fascinating hobby that has evolved over centuries. The idea of making an environment that supports life and is aesthetically appealing is an exciting quest for many people. Technology has evolved to support more species, in cleaner and longer lasting environments.

This book will give you the facts to start your own aquarium and learn aquascaping freshwater and salt water tanks from styles and design to set up with planting, lighting, substrates, coral, and ornaments including live rock. You will also gain the knowledge of the nitrogen cycle and water testing for aquarium maintenance.

1. Aquascaping

Aquascaping is an exciting outlet for imagination and learning that results in a living creation. This art involves the parameters of design, the knowledge of particular biology, and an awareness of available technology.

Aquascaping began with keeping fish in aquariums. The first aquariums are dated well over four thousand years ago with records by the Sumerians in Egypt and Assyria. These aquariums were man-made ponds rather than the glass enclosures of today.

The first fish breeding in captivity is attributed to the Chinese over twenty centuries later, when they farmed carp. Japan then started selective breeding of decorative goldfish.

Not until the eighteenth century did we learn about the oxygen requirements of living creatures and create the "Balanced Aquarium." The Balanced Aquarium included an open water surface and plants for providing oxygen. Later in mid-century there is the first evidence of the word "aquarium," attributed to Philip Gosse, a British naturalist.

In 1853, the first public aquarium was built in London. A founder of the Barnum and Bailey circus, P.T. Barnum opened the first aquarium soon after at the American

Museum in New York City. Other cities began building public aquariums and today they are found worldwide.

Large public aquariums often involve aquascaping in their displays. Many public aquariums exhibit wildlife from a certain natural habitat which makes these biotope aquascapes. There are many aquariums around the U.S. including the Alaska Sea Life Canter, Denver Downtown Aquarium, the Florida Aquarium, the Mote Marine Laboratory and Aquarium, Maui Ocean Center, the Waikiki Aquarium, Audubon Aquarium of the Americas, the National Aquarium Baltimore, Albuquerque Aquarium, Dallas Aquarium and many more.

In the first part of the nineteenth century, aeration and charcoal filtration was used in aquariums and in the 1950s - the under gravel filter began to be used. The under gravel filter is said to be the aquarium's greatest invention.

Then in 1984, the wet/dry filter was introduced, which is the second greatest advancement in aquariums. This enabled sustaining fish, corals, and invertebrates in aquariums.

Aquascaping is the art of positioning rocks, stones, plants, driftwood, and coral in an aquarium. Aquascaping has become a hobby and craft on its own—underwater gardening. Aquascaping is a learned art form for creating enchanting underwater landscapes. Many replicate underwater scenes and others natural scenes such as deserts, waterfalls, mountains, forests, jungles, and so on.

While the primary goal aquascaping is to create a pleasing aesthetic environment, there are numerous landscape technical aspects to be considered. Aquatic plant maintenance, filtration, supporting carbon dioxide levels to sustain underwater photosynthesis, substrate and fertilization, any fish or other creatures that will be sharing the environment, lighting, and algae management. Aquascapes typically share environments with fish and plants, yet they can also be plants only, plants and rocks, or rocks and no plants.

Aquascaping requires knowledge of plants and aquarium basics including the temperature and lighting requirements of specific plants, water chemistry, substrates, and design principles. This knowledge and experience will allow you to experiment and use more materials and plant types as well as create more complex and stunning aquascapes as you progress.

Plants such as corals and many fish can be expensive. You will save life and money by knowing how to create the idyllic environment and maintain it. Learning about the requirements of aquarium life, the aquascape styles, and how to plan an aquascape will reduce or eliminate frustration and help you construct pleasing creations. Success with your aquarium will depend on how much you understand and being certain to provide for the needs of your aquarium's inhabitants.

2. Aquascaping Styles

There are several distinct styles of aquascaping design with varying degrees of creating, balancing, and maintenance challenges.

Dutch Style

Source: gwapa.org

The Dutch style is a lush array where different kinds of plants with assorted leaf colors, sizes, and textures are presented. The Dutch style originated in the Netherlands in the 1930s in freshwater aquariums. Today, Dutch aquascapes are still generally created in freshwater systems because there are few ornamental plants that grow in saltwater aquariums.

Plants are commonly located on varying raised terraces in a linear row fashion of left-to-right known as "Dutch streets." These often do not include any rocks or driftwood. There are typically smartly trimmed collections of plants that have feathery foliage. While many plants are used, this style commonly includes Limnophila aquatic, Hygrophila, Alternanthera reineckii with red leaves, Ammania gracilis, and Rotala. Most of the floor is covered and tall plants often line the back side.

Japanese Style

Source: http://freshwater-aquarium-passion.blogspot.com/

Iwagumi aquascapes belong to the Nature Aquarium style category. Iwagumi means "rock formation" and how these rocks are positioned as well as their number has meaning.

The Japanese style or nature aquarium was introduced in the 1990s by Takashi Amano. Takashi Amano set new standards of aquarium creations and management. Amano's <u>Nature Aquarium World</u> gained international attention and spawned a wave of interest in aquascaping.

Amano modeled aquascapes after intricate Japanese gardening techniques to replicate natural landscapes with a theme of tranquility and simplicity. They imitate miniature landscapes with arrangements of asymmetrical groups including a few species of plants and stones or driftwood.

With simplicity in mind, colors are limited and Iwagumi aquascapes usually have one kind of carpeting plant (glosso, hair grass, or hemianthus callitrichoides.) Small leaf plants are sometimes included such as Eleocharis acicularis, Glossostigma elatinoides, or Hemianthus callitrichoides.

Riccia fluitans, small aquatic ferns, and Java moss (Versicularia dubyana or Taxiphyllum barbieri) are regularly highlighted.

Amano's style uses techniques from the Japanese aesthetic ideas of Wabi-sabi and Iwagumi . Wabi-sabi centers on transience and minimalism to create beauty and Iwagumi dictates rock arrangement. In Iwagumi, the main stone is called the Oyaishi and located off-center and the Soeishi, or complementary stones, are arranged nearby. The secondary stones known as Fukuseki are placed in subordinate spots.

The central point of the Iwagumi aquascape is established by the asymmetric location of the Oyaishi with ratios that involve Pythagorean tuning.

A common iwagumi style is the sanzon iwagumi style. Sanzon stands for "three pillars" in Japanese. This style uses three stones with one being noticeably larger than the other two. This arrangement symbolizes Buddhism whereas the central stone is flanked by the smaller ones, sometimes pointing toward the larger stone as if bowing.

Iwagumi aquascape aquariums with fish typically include only one species. These are schooling fish such as tetras, cardinal tetras, or harlequin rasboras.

Maintaining an Iwagumi aquascape is more difficult than most other styles because of the limits of a single plant species and the required light levels. The carpeting plants used grow slowly and getting fertilizer levels correct is difficult. Algae are common and stem plants are not used to help achieve balance. Amano or other fresh water shrimp species (such as Caridina multidentata and Neocaridina heteropoda) are frequently introduced to help reduce the algae. Iwagumi aquascaped aquariums are not recommended for beginners.

Biotope

Source: http://freshwater-aquarium-passion.blogspot.com/2010/12/aga-aquascaping-contest-2010-results.html

The word biotope comes from the German word "Biotop" which originated from the Greek word 'bios.' The definition of bios is 'life or organism'. Topos is 'a place.' So biotope means *a place where life lives*. The results of biotope aquascaping can be very aesthetically pleasing.

A biotope aquascape strives to imitate the environment of a geographic location. The same water conditions (temperature and chemistry), plants and fish species found at the locations, and identical gravel or substrate are used. This makes the specific requirements of the aquarium well defined. There is no need to research or experiment to determine the compatibility of plants and creatures. Plants and fish do not have to be included, but if they are, they must be the same as what is in the natural habitat.

Replicating a natural environment includes knowing the water temperature and hardness, the natural species of

21

plants and fish, and lighting conditions. A biotope aquarium is confined to the elements of the precise natural environment for aquascaping. However having a set of parameters can make balancing the life in the aquarium easier and give you and observers a look through a window into a natural setting.

Biotopes have been created by biologists and scientists to study areas of the world for future preservation and protection. Replicating some locations can be more difficult than others; research to see what others have done before you choose a place to imitate. Live aquarium plants are often easier to maintain than a non-planted aquarium as the quality of aeration, filtration, food, and algae management is frequently better.

Jungle Style

Source: stevenchong-no-gmf.deviantart.com

The Jungle style is usually densely planted much like its name. Plants are commonly green foliage, though some have more color. The light shines down from above as happens in the natural environment it mimics.

There are often low green plants in the front and coarser leaf shapes included such as Echinodorus bleheri.

Paludariums

Source: http://blog.aquascape.co.in/?p=10

A paludarium is an aquascape where a portion of the terrestrial contents such as plants and rocks and or other items are above the water while the remainder is submerged. Paludariums are common for aquariums containing amphibians but can support a variety of species including fish, snakes, frogs, newts and crabs. They imitate swamps, flooded forests, beaches, coastlines, islands and river, lake and pond edges. This style works well for some biotope themes. Some are only partially filled with water.

The substrate is built up to form an area that is above the water line which allows plants, such as Cyperus alternifolius, Spathiphyllum wallisii, and some bromeliads, to grow with roots immersed under the water. Rocks and wood can also rise above the water's surface.

Reef Style

Reef style aquascapes are indicative of their label as they replicate natural reefs. While the Dutch and Nature styles are typically freshwater aquariums, the reef style is created in a salt water system. The Reef style is based on live rock arrangements and often includes corals and additional marine invertebrates along with coralline algae, as few ornamental plants live in salt water.

Algae are undesirable for aquascaping. Algae can be managed by lighting and creatures such as shrimp and snails that eat algae. Correct light and CO_2 help preferred plants grow and control nutrient levels, to make certain the plants make use of all fertilizer so there is none to sustain algae.

There are 'aquascapers' who employ significant equipment for CO_2 balance as well as lighting and filtration and there are those that curtail the use of technology. A "natural planted tank" is an approach popularized by Diana Walstad. She is the technical advisor for the AGA (Aquatic Gardeners Association). Diana's concept advocates using soil instead of aquarium gravel, no CO_2 apparatus and restricted lighting. Few fish are included to minimize fish waste and plants perform the water filtration using fish waste for fertilizer.

Lighting is a significant factor for the reef style aquascape. Well-designed lighting will not only help show off corals in many shapes and bright colors, but a few that contain symbiotic fluorescent algae-like protozoa called zooxanthellae can be beautifully highlighted. Ultraviolet light aids the health of these invertebrates, and enhances the colors these fluorescent microorganisms emit.

Black Water Style

Image source: practicalfishkeeping.co.uk

A black water aquascape is a biotope designed to imitate a particular area with murky waters and dead plant matter that represents a swamp. Blackwater aquariums are not as common but can be very attractive in their own right. They often have amber, earthy, warm colors that match other earthen tones of interior design.

The secret to a black water aquarium is in the dead leaves, rich soil, and fallen branches. These are a source of tannin. The carbon filter is reduced or not used in the pump.

3. Aquascaping Design Elements

Aquascaping does involve your imagination and creativity. However there are several formulas and theories of design you can use to build an aesthetically pleasing aquascape. As you learn, you can you can experiment and remove items and start over if you develop a better idea.

Focal Point

The goal of aquascaping is to create pleasing and interesting designs. Where you focus attention is how you can control the way people see your aquascape. The focal point draws the gaze of the viewer first and then their eyes move to explore the aquascape.

- A focal point can be a rock, rock formation, particular plant, or a piece of driftwood that draws the attention.
- There should be only one focal point. The exception is very large tanks.
- Every aquascape style should have a focal point.
- The focal point must be placed correctly according to the Golden Rule of aquascaping.

The Golden Rule (or Ratio) of Aquascaping

The Golden Rule or Ratio of Aquascaping comes from the Greeks. This is the theory that the ratio 1:1.618 is the most pleasing to the human eye. In other words, by making the focal point slightly off center, rather than in dead center, you guide the observer's eyes rather than allowing them to wander back and forth. This rule is used in many designs and art forms.

Source: www.freshwateraquariumplants.com

Use a tape measure (or ruler) and a calculator and measure the length of the tank from end to end. Divide your results by 2.618. Now use that number to measure from one end of the tank toward the middle. That is where you place your focal point.

Example:

- Your tank is 40 inches wide.
- 40 divided by 2.618 is 15.28 inches.
- Measure 15.28 inches from one side or the other of the tank for determining your focal point.

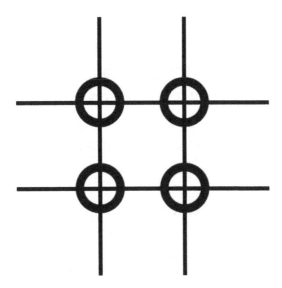

The Rule of Thirds

The "Rule of Thirds" is another method of design theory that derives from the Golden Rule or Ratio, which was discovered by the ancient Greeks. This rule has been applied in every art form for centuries. The rule of thirds gives shows us how to locate elements in an aquascape that helps direct the eyes.

Here is how this works: Imagine your aquascape divided into nine equal parts separated by two equally spaced horizontal lines and two equally spaced vertical lines, as in the image. Your significant elements ought to be located either on these lines or at the red-circled intersections.

By arranging items with the rule of thirds we can create appealing and interesting designs; aquascapes that move your viewers' eyes in a flowing manner revealing beauty with direction. The rule of thirds is another aid to help you establish where to place the focal point and secondary points of interest to create a fascinating viewing experience for your friends, family, and guests.

Foreground, Middle, and Background

Establishing a distinct foreground, middle, and background will help you design. Often, somewhat gradual transference between these sections is more appealing. Rocks and wood in the middle ground that graduate in height toward the background is appealing. A balance of open space can be dramatic and bring more attention to ornaments, plants, and the overall design.

There is a fine line between simple and boring. Keep things simple and do not overcrowd your tank. However use variety such as more than one type of plant to keep from being boring. Too many large leaf plants or large rocks can cause your aquascape to appear smaller.

Symmetry

Symmetry is not a goal for aquascape design. Symmetry causes your aquascape to look unnatural or too structured.

Shape

Filling in your background is not always the best idea. Placing high plants in the background can cause an unnatural 'hedge' look. Creating shapes and curves will look much better.

There are several design shapes to choose from. A convex shape creates a pleasing aesthetic element. You can use rocks or wood to do this. The concave shape can also look terrific and can be accomplished with rocks, wood or by trimming plants. A triangular design is often unique and appealing. An island design is fun and can look very interesting.

Mountain 'Scapes'

There are several useful tips for creating mountains:

- Use the Golden Ratio for locating your mountain in your scene.
- Plants in the foreground should be low to the ground.
- Make the beginning third of your mountain from the ground very steep or even vertical.

- Be consistent with one type of rock to create mountains.
- Pile substrate at the base to create the natural appearance of the mountain rising from the floor.

Planting with Design in Mind

When planting start with the background plants first and work forward. Place plants densely with stems in the substrate at about an inch apart. Moss can be tied to objects such as rock or wood for an optimum result but use sparingly because most will grow fast.

Separate plant types into different areas. Different textured and varied green shades of plants add depth and interest to the look. Colorful plants such as red and orange can add to your scheme, but consider whether locations will be competing with your focal point.

Carpet Plants for Freshwater Aquascapes

Pygmy Chain Sword

Pygmy chain sword is popular and resembles common grass which is brilliant for imitating lawns or land.

Image source: Shrimptank.ca

Hairgrass

Hairgrass is close to Pygmy Sword, although thinner and more delicate and tends to move with the water.

Image source: Aquascapingworld.com

Dwarf Baby Tears

Dwarf baby tears are small and stay that way. They lend themselves to imaginative uses such as even treetops.

Image source: Aquaticplantcentral.com

Java Moss

Java moss is very delicate and looks like mold. When grown on wood, this can resemble and mimic a tree.

Image source: Killies.com

Marsilea Minuta

Image source: Azaquaticplants.com

Marsila Minuta has a vibrant green color that looks like clover.

Planning an Iwagumi Aquascape

Iwagumi aquascapes are inviting with their simple tranquility and beauty, yet creating them can be difficult and require patience. They are often composed on just one or two carpeting plant species that grow very slowly. The balance is delicate and frequently algae overtake the scenery before the intended plants.

Many Iwagumi hobbyists use stem or floating plants to consume excess nutrients and release inhibitors that slow algae growth. Hornwort or a hygrophila species will work. They often remove these plants when their carpeting plants are flourishing. Fertilizing should be limited during this period. If algae do take hold, reduce lighting time and fertilizer.

Other Considerations

Think about the location of your aquascape. The setting for your aquascape is a consideration for the style and colors you choose. For example a room of modern furnishings in black and white with only a few dashes of color might call for a simple Iwagumi aquascape while a cabin atmosphere with earth tones might be better served with a biotope or black water style tank.

Aquascape Contests

The Dutch are credited with starting aquascape contests. The judging was stringent requiring judges to attend three years of training and testing. The Dutch still hold the competitions beginning at the local levels and advancing to nationals. Criteria judged include composition and the biological health for fish, plants, and water. Judges visit tanks at the home of contestants. The National Aquarium Society oversees the event.

The Aquatic Gardeners Association of the U. S., Aqua Design Amano of Japan, and AquaticScapers Europe, hold freshwater aquascaping contests as well. The

Aquatic Gardeners Association contest is judged based on:

- overall impression (35 points)
- composition, balance, use of space and use of color (30 points)
- selection and materials (20 points)
- viability of aquascape (15 points)

Acuavida in Spain, the Greek Aquarist's Club, and France's Aquagora also hold contests.

4. Lighting

Choosing lighting for your aquascape involves much more than aesthetic appeal. Aquarium lights are not only for your viewing pleasure; they provide live plants and corals with illumination to manufacture their food. Plants, corals and other inhabitants depend on lighting to produce food. Too much light can offset the balance of your environment and cause algae growth and too little light can cause the demise of living plants and creatures.

Even the most basic aquarium kits usually include lights and a tank hood. The lights included might or might not be appropriate for your plan. The tank hood is for preventing water from evaporating, keeping dust and foreign items out of the water, and for housing lights. The right lighting system will help you control the amount of light your habitat receives and for how long each day.

Photosynthesis and Respiration

Photosynthesis and respiration are the two processes that occur in plants. They are necessary for healthy plants to break down nutrients and grow. These processes occur during the phases of the cycle of light and dark. Just like light and dark, photosynthesis and respiration are polar opposites. Photosynthesis happens with the light and respiration occurs after photosynthesis in the dark. Photosynthesis supports the food chain and is required for all life on earth. Your aquascape must mimic the amount of light and darkness naturally required by the plants. Depending on where a specific plant species evolved, a specific light or darkness period will be optimal.

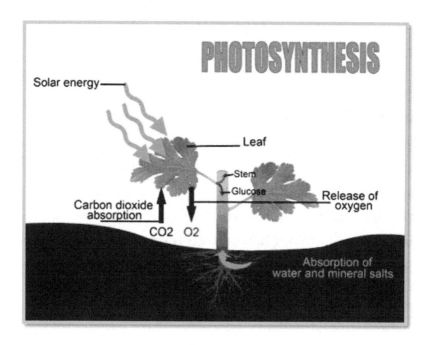

Oxygen and carbon dioxide are by products of the two plant processes. When plants are exposed to light, the carbon dioxide is absorbed by the plant mainly through the leaves and oxygen is expelled. The mixture of carbon, hydrogen and oxygen molecules chemically merge with the plant's chlorophyll-causing simple sugars to be produced. Light activates the chlorophyll resulting in photosynthesis. During the respiration process, the food is broken down. Food with oxygen and energy is released as heat along with carbon dioxide.

Light Timers

Many types of light generate heat and can cause your water temperature to get too high and cook the inhabitants. Leaving lights on too long everyday can promote algae growth. The lights in your tank should usually mimic the natural environment and, in most cases, this is six to twelve hours a day. A lighting system with a timer will help you maintain the correct light exposure. A light timer gives you one less thing to remember each day. Many tank hoods have either built in lights with timers or separate power cords for timer additions. Fish and other inhabitants also appreciate the cycle of light and dark.

There are hoods that incorporate several types of lighting such as an actinic (blue light) bulb, a full spectrum bulb and a moon light. A timer can be used to schedule each light simulating the lighting during dawn and twilight periods. A moon light with a desirable effect can be scheduled for night.

Types of Lighting

Correct and adequate lighting is imperative for achieving balance and continued success. There are many types of fish tank lighting available. The type of light you need depends on your tank type and inhabitants. Freshwater and saltwater tanks that only contain fish can often get by with the regular fluorescent lights. That is not true for most tanks that contain live aquascapes whether freshwater or saltwater.

Light types include:

- Fluorescent Lights
- Compact Fluorescent Lights
- High Output (HP) or T5-HO Fluorescent
- High Output (VHO) Fluorescent
- Light Emitting Diodes (LED)
- Metal Halide Lights

Aquarium Light Spectrum

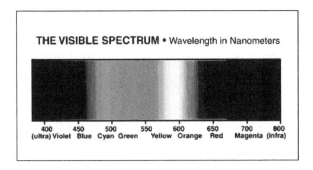

Spectrum of visible light expressed in nanometers (nm). A nanometer is equal to one billionth of a meter and references the wavelength of light in an aquarium. Varying wavelengths generate different colors. Our eyes can only see light from 380 nm (violet) to 780 nm (red).

Regular Fluorescent Light

Basic florescent lights are the inexpensive ones that come with most starter aquariums. They normally range from 15 to 40 watts with Kelvin ratings from 3,000° to 10,000°. (The Kelvin scale measures the color temperature.)

Compact Fluorescent Light Bulb

Compact is the next level up of fluorescent lights. They range from 10 to 100 watts with Kelvin ratings from 5,000° to 10,000°. These lights are brighter and more intense. These compact lights should only be used with special fans and vented hoods due to the amount of heat they produce.

High Output (HP) or T5-HO Fluorescent Light

HO Fluorescent lights range from 20-60 watts with Kelvin ratings from 6,000° to 11,000°. They last longer and cost more than the basic fluorescent lights that come with the starter aquariums. These lights use a T5 light fixture and they frequently include built in fans that keep bulbs working at the most favorable levels. T5-HO lights supply an abundance of light and are cooler than metal halides. T5 fluorescent lights are smaller and brighter than the T8 fluorescents.

T5-HO lights help grow some of the most demanding SPS corals when placed in the center to upper regions of the aquarium. They give off an even lighting, which is good for plant health.

Very High Output (VHO) Fluorescent Light

VHO Fluorescent lights are not as popular as the other types and range from 75 to 160 watts with Kelvin ratings from 10,000° to 20,000°. They are more costly and produce a great deal of heat so the fixtures have built in fans. The fans are sometimes not enough to keep water from overheating and require an aquarium chiller. You need a ballast or a specific fixture made for VHO lights.

Metal Halide Light

Metal Halide lamps range from 175 to 1000 watts with Kelvin ratings from 5,000° to 20,000°. They are very bright and the most comparable to the sun in terms of luminosity but can become very hot and need fan cooling. Larger tanks do better with Halides.

LED Aquarium Light

Light-emitting diodes (LEDs) make light by converting electric current. LEDs are more efficient than standard incandescent bulbs: According to the U.S. Department of Energy, a typical Energy Star-rated LED uses 20 to 25 percent of the energy that an incandescent bulb uses; the LED lasts up to 25 times longer.[1]

LED lights are pricey but offer several distinct advantages over other types of lights. The advantages of LED lights over traditional fluorescent and metal halide lights include:

- Much longer life span
- Cooler operation
- Less energy consumption
- No filament to break
- Flexibility in configurations due to the small size

---

[1] U.S. Department of Energy: Frequently Asked Questions: Lighting Choices to Save You Money; February 2011

- Better LED fixtures let you customize colors and light intensity on programmed schedules.

Moon lights are generally LED lights.

Freshwater Aquarium Light - Fish Only

Low watt Fluorescent lights between 18 and 40 watts work well for aquascapes with no live plants.

Freshwater Aquarium Plant Lighting

Choosing a fresh water plant lighting systems is dependent on the:

- size and depth of the tank
- types of plants
- growth rate desired

A common measurement is two to five watts per aquarium gallon. Know how many gallons your tank holds, the light wattage, and how much light your specific plants require.

Saltwater Aquarium Light - Fish Only

Saltwater tanks supporting only fish are fine with regular Fluorescent bulbs. A full spectrum light is desirable with a bulb of 6,000 K and an actinic (blue light) bulb. If you want coralline algae to grow, some grow better with more actinic lighting and low phosphate levels.

Saltwater Reef Aquarium Light

Lighting a salt water tank can be the most expensive investment at start-up and will add to the electric bill and require buying replacement bulbs in the future. Saltwater reef tanks that contain corals and other life forms that need light require high output (HP), very high output (VHO) fluorescent, metal halide lamps, or a combination of all. These lighting systems often create enough heat to warrant the need of an aquarium chiller.

A common recommendation for reef tanks is between 4 and 10 watts per tank gallon though you need to learn the light requirements for each species you are considering. Most of the coral utilize zooxanthellae and photosynthesis to supply food. Some corals are also filter feeders, but this is usually less of a contributor to their nutritional needs.

- For soft coral, use power compacts when aquarium depth is 24 inches deep or less.
- For the large stony coral, use HO or VHO fluorescents.
- For small stony coral, use T5-HO Fluorescents or Metal Halides. Metal halides are a good choice, although they heat the water. The T5-HO lights produce less heat and are less costly.

Keep in mind that the deeper you go in water, the less light penetrates, so locating corals higher in your aquascape will get them additional light.

Bulbs and Tubes

Choosing the right bulbs is imperative for optimum coral, plant health and aesthetics.

A Kelvin is a measurement of temperature. Your goal should be 6500 kelvin (about what the sun is) or more. 10,000 kelvins produces a nice white glow. Less than 6000 kelvins causes an unwanted yellowish tint and anything above 10,000 kelvins has no further effect on coral or plant growth.

T5-HO emitting between 7,000 kelvins and 10,000 kelvins is the optimum spectrum while with metal halides aim for 10,000 kelvins.

The light a bulb generates can be measured in lumens. The electrical power that supplies the light bulb is measured in watts.

Lumens are a measurement of the total output of a light source. Lux is a measurement of the intensity of the light. Sunlight is about 32,000 lux. A lux meter is a device that measures the 'lux', or light intensity in an aquarium. A lux meter can tell you if your light system can provide adequate lux for your corals and the best place to locate them. While 2 watts per gallon is usually enough, 4 watts per gallon is desirable.

Conversions:

40 watt incandescent bulb = 450 lumens

60 watt incandescent bulb = 800 lumens

100 watt incandescent bulb = 1600 lumens

The technology of LED bulbs results in a higher ratio of lumens to watts than incandescent bulbs. Lumens do not define light quality, color, or tone.

Plants and Light

There are some general signs that your plants might have problems related to light:

- Low crouched growth can be caused by too much blue in the light spectrum.
- Tall gangling plants can be caused by too much red in the light spectrum.
- Stunted growth usually means too much green and yellow in the light spectrum.

When plants are not getting enough light symptoms can include pale green or yellowish color instead of bright or dark green, weak stems, few leaves growing, better growth on plants near the light source.

Diatom algae is also a sign that the daily light period is too short; lights are aging and have lost spectrum; floating or other plants are blocking light, or light levels are too low.

Electrical Safety

Most of us have heard since childhood that electricity and water do not mix and can be fatal. This is a constant consideration with aquariums.

Always turn off and unplug all electrical appliances before making contact with the water. That means do not stick your hands in the water unless all electrical systems are off and unplugged.

Not much current is needed to cause an electrical shock. Only 10 milliamps can cause pain and anything over 50 milliamps can kill you. A heater can be drawing 800 milliamps.

A core balance earth leakage circuit breaker (ELCB) can be installed in some wiring systems to monitor the current and break the circuit, should a short or fault occur.

In the United States and Canada, these are commonly known as a Ground Fault Circuit Interrupter (GFCI),

Ground Fault Interrupter (GFI) or an Appliance Leakage Current Interrupter (ALCI).

In the United Kingdom, these devices are referred to as a RCD or a RCBO. Non residual-current circuit protection devices are called Circuit Breakers or MCBs and sometimes called trips or trip switches.

In Australia, the devices are known as safety switches or a RCD.

All of them are designed to break the circuit when the current loss exceeds a certain point. This cut-off point range is from 10 milliamps to 30 milliamps, and 30 milliamps is suitable for an aquarium.

5. Substrate

The substrate is the foundation of your aquascape. You want to get this right from the beginning as replacing a substrate usually means complete disassembly of your tank. Learn what nutrients your choice of plants will need to decide on a substrate as plants feed from the roots. There are plants that require specific substrates. The symptoms of the wrong substrate will often not show immediately, but can destroy your aquascape. A substrate designed for salt water tanks can release salts and minerals into the water that can imbalance pH levels and be fatal to some fresh water plants and inhabitants such as Discus and some Asian fish, as well as a variety of plants including moss, Fissidens, and floating plants.

The substrate helps anchor and provides nutrients for your plants. Live aquarium plants improve quality of aeration, filtration, nutrients, algae management and the health of inhabitants.

Because the substrate is feeding your plants, you need to choose one that is rich in the macronutrients. Plants suffering from deficiencies can discolor and die. You can help supplement your plant diet with specific fertilizers, but they can cause other imbalances and you cannot make up for a deficient substrate.

A substrate is best when three to eight millimeters per grain. S substrate grain that is too small can suffocate plant roots. A substrate that is too large can reduce root contact. Also, consider all other live residents of your aquascape when considering substrates. Read the labels on the substrate packaging.

Substrates include:

ADA Aquasoil – Excellent for plants but can lower pH balance.

Clay – Clay is great as a bottom layer substrate for specific plants though can be difficult to work with and is not recommended for beginners.

Plain Gravel – This is not a good choice unless at least half of the total volume is a nutrient-rich supplement or soil.

Fluorite/Seachem – Excellent sources of nutrients for plants.

Soil – Soil is an excellent choice and inexpensive. Avoid any soil that contains fertilizers or phosphates that could be harmful to your aquarium.

Commercial substrates such as Eco Complete or Up Aqua work well. As with all substrates, find out how they affect water or pH balance and plants. There are also additives in tab or pellet form that are placed close to the roots of plants that work.

Aquarium Sand

There is a variety of aquarium sands available including live sand and dry sand. Consider the grain size of any sand, for if the grain is too small harmful gasses can be trapped in the substrate. Grains that are too large can collect detritus. A grain size from 1mm to 2mm is recommended.

"Live sand" promoters tout that living beneficial bacteria are in the sand which is questionable.

Sand must be cleaned before use. A five gallon bucket filled up to halfway with the sand and then with tap water is a great way to clean sand. By stirring the sand the lighter impurities and dirt will rise and can be drained. You may need to repeat this process several times until the water is no longer visibly dirty or too cloudy.

A shallow sand bed under 2 inches deep or a deep sand bed of over 4 inches deep will help prevent algae growth on the sand bed. If you use a shallow sand bed, including live rock can aid in nitrogen balance. When your sand bed is in place, let your aquascape settle for 24 hours or more.

Liquid Fertilizers

There are two main groups of fertilizers; macronutrients and micronutrients.

Macronutrients – This group includes nitrogen, potassium and phosphorous, and are generally found in water with fish. If your aquascape contains numerous plants you will need to add macronutrients.

Micronutrients – These include iron Boron, Calcium, Chloride, Copper, Iron, Magnesium, Manganese, Molybdenum, Sulfur and Zinc. These are found in commercial fertilizers. Certain plants might need an additional iron supplement.

Seachem Flourish and NPK – These products are effective, but costly.

Homemade – Some websites and guides suggest making fertilizers. If you choose to make your own, research all ingredients and nutrients as well as the quantities to prevent harming any other tank inhabitants.

PMDD (Poor Man's Daily Drops) – A Sears and Cronin recipe that works. You can make this quickly and for little cost. You can also buy the dry mix.

Iron – As mentioned, an iron additive will help plants stay healthy and colorful.

The lighting and CO2 are factors in determining quantities of fertilizer needed.

Ornaments

Ornaments are the wood and rocks in your aquascape. Many hobbyists consider the ornaments to be the heart of the aquascape.

Wood

Appealing wood usually has branches or twigs that attract and direct the eyes. Wood can have a dramatic effect on your scene and it is an element that can spark your imagination and creativity. Wood that seems to climb your aquascape with interesting bends is desirable. You can intertwine these with plants and moss as well.

Wood can rise up from the bottom as if it was once growing or come down from the top as if the branch fell from a shoreline. Wood can be placed so that some is submerged while the rest is above the surface.

Be certain to boil any wood you find before placing the piece in your tank. If you purchase wood, always wash the piece before using to remove any chemicals that could have been used for wood treatment.

You might find a perfect piece of wood that will not stay where you want. The wood might be too buoyant and float to the top. The wood might need to soak in water and become saturated first. Soaking wood (outside your tank) will help remove the natural tannins that can offset pH balance. There are woods that saturate quickly such as the popular aquarium wood Manzanita. Some pieces might need to be weighed or tied down. If you use any silicone to hold pieces together, make sure it is non-toxic.

Rocks

Rocks are another element for creative venture in aquascaping. Rocks of natural colors are preferred and - of course - those that are naturally found in the location a biotope is imitating are a must. Earth tone rocks such as black, grey, and browns usually look best.

Source: ggftw.com

Any rock you choose must stand up to being submerged in water. A rock that crumbles causes disorder in your scene. Make sure all loose particles and dirt have been removed from rocks first. Use a stiff brush to scrub rocks and let them soak overnight in a bucket or sink.

Shale

Shale can contain a high content of organic matter which can release hydrocarbons (petroleum) into the water. This will cause an oily scum to appear on your water's surface.

Any rock that will affect the environment of your aquascape negatively should be avoided.

Limestone

Carbonate rocks such as limestone can increase the pH and hardness of your water. However limestone does not seem to significantly increase pH. So while carbonate rocks can upset pH, they are not always a danger - depending on what else you have in your tank. For example, the African Rift Lake Cichlid benefits from the pH. Check your pH weekly if you use any carbonate rocks.

Carbonate Rocks

There is a quick test for identifying carbonate rocks called the 'acid test'. Some people use vinegar for this test by dropping some on the rock and checking for bubbles or fizz. Bubbles present are a positive sign of a carbonate rock. However, vinegar is a weak acid and will not determine the status of all rocks. You need diluted hydrochloric acid, for accurate results.

Do not make contact with hydrochloric or muriatic acid. Protect yourself with gloves, long sleeves and pants and safety glasses or goggles.

Pyrite or Fool's Gold

Pyrite should be avoided in aquascapes and any aquariums because of a strong acidifying effect, possible dangerous heavy metal content, and the acidifying effect it can have on water, causing heavy metals to be toxic.

Pyrite resembles gold, hence the name 'fool's gold.' Pyrite has a yellow shiny metallic luster with crystals and often sharp edges. Pyrite can be contained within other rocks and appears as spots or streaks on the surface.

Heavy Metals

Heavy metals (lead, zinc, copper, cadmium, iron and so on) are toxic for fish, inverts, and people. Some rocks can inject heavy-metal pollutants into your water. The chances are slim, but there are ways to make those chances even less.

If you collect rocks, then review the area where they come from. Avoid rocks from old mining areas or landfills as well as downstream from mines or landfills. Also avoid areas where heavy manufacturing or chemical manufacturing is occurring or has taken place.

Metals are mostly dangerous to fish only when in a free ionic state in the water. Water conditioners 'detoxify' heavy metals by binding them with compounds that fish cannot take in. Heavy metals are often locked in these compounds and rendered inert. However, acidic water (with a pH of lower than 7) can activate dangerous metals.

Iron is the most common metal present in nature as rust. This iron oxide can sometimes be seen on rocks. This is usually not an issue unless there is enough iron oxide that the water begins to discolor with a rusty tint.

Generally Safe Rocks

- Crystalline Quartz (Rock Crystal, Amethyst, Citrine, Rose Quartz, Smokey Quartz).
- Granite
- Microcrystalline Quartz (Jasper, Agate, and Sard).
- Jade
- Petrified wood
- Onyx Black rock
- Slate
- Quartz

Unsafe or Caution Rocks

- Coal
- Dolomite
- Limestone
- Sandstone
- Carbonate rocks
- Pyrite or Fool's Gold

Live Rock

Aquascaping with live rock in a saltwater environment adds to aesthetic appeal and the health of marine life. Live rock can help filtrate the water in your tank. Rock can also be utilized to obscure heaters, pumps and other equipment.

Place rock with the aquascape goals of optimizing filtration, maintaining a functional and safe environment for the inhabitants, and satisfying your aesthetic vision.

Rock is a natural item usually in a natural state and shape. Open type structures are desirable to allow for water movement around the rocks, help keep rocks free of detritus build up, and provide any fish with hiding spots. Fish seek hiding areas to feel secure which reduces any stress.

Become familiar with the types of rock available and their appearance, color, shapes, sizes, and weights in order to visualize your design. This will make choosing rock easier and you will have a better chance of achieving your vision. You can create stacks, overhangs, pillars, crests, peaks, and caves. Emulating nature scenes will usually be the most visually appealing. Review natural pictures of rock formations on land and underwater to get ideas.

Plan the foundations for your rock structures. Rocks can rest on the substrate, the floor of your tank or be built up with underwater epoxy. Be careful about placing rocks on top of some substrates as certain fish burrow and can cause rocks to move and or fall. You can bind rocks together with ties, underwater epoxy or use gravity to stack them. Keep in mind the environment is wet and fluid so rocks can slide or fall. Falling rock can injure fish, damage plants and even crack or break glass. Using the sides of your tank to support a rock structure is not recommended. This reduces the benefit of filtration and can cause glass damage.

Rocks can be flat on the aquarium bottom to replicate a reef or piled to resemble upper reef slopes. They can also be stacked high at the back of the tank to mimic reef walls or slopes.

Rock with little or no coralline algae works well as base rock for your structure's foundation. Rock that is covered with coralline can be attractive and often shows better at the higher levels of your arrangement. Coralline rocks should be placed where they will receive light.

Generally you can use up to one and a half pounds of rock per gallon of water. Of course this varies with the sizes, shapes, and types of rock you use. Do not overdo rock in your aquarium and allow adequate room for water movement, filtration and fish as well as other residents. Using more than one type of rock can make your scene more interesting and introduce additional beneficial bacteria into the environment.

Sort rock into three categories:

Flat Rocks: These rocks can be used as cliffs, bridge pieces, slopes or walls.

Support or Leg Rocks: These rocks can support other rocks.

Larger Bulky Rocks: These rocks can serve as legs or supports, bridge pieces, faces, slopes, or mountains.

You can also incorporate coral into your rock structures. Because corals need different amounts of light and water movement, the design ought to allow for this. Take into consideration that different types of corals have specific light needs and that some corals should not be placed in contact with other types of corals as they can sting one another.

6. Coral

Aquarium coral can be found in many colors, shapes, types and sizes. There are SPS (Small Polyped Stony) corals that have restrictive water requirements and LPS (Large Polyp Stonycorals) that have less limiting needs. Some of these coral require different temperatures and more light than others. By deciding what type of corals you want you can then determine the right equipment you will need.

All new corals require a coral dip or - better yet - a quarantine time before being placed in your tank. This will help you avoid the coral pests that can invade your aquarium. Creating and maintaining a tank with healthy coral is the height of reef aquarium accomplishment.

Acanthastrea Coral

Source: http://blog.aquanerd.com

Scientific Name: Acanthastrea spp.

Common Names: Acans, Moon coral

Degree of Difficulty: Fairly Easy. Acanthastrea coral needs to be well fed with scheduled target feedings. Feed them mysis, brine shrimp, minced oysters or clams in the dark when tentacles are extended.

pH : 8.2 - 8.4
Temperature: 75°F - 82°F (24°C - 28°C)
Water Hardness: 8° to 12° dH
Calcium: 400 - 450 ppm

Origin: Indo-Pacific, Australia

Lighting: Moderate: power compacts, T5's and Metal Halides. To acclimate them to the light place them at the bottom of the tank to start.

Water Movement: Moderate flow

Frag: Cut the corallite below the polyp and join to a frag plug. Maintain favorable saltwater conditions when feeding them.

Acropora Coral

Source:
http://www.aquariumdomain.com/viewCoralSpecies.php?coral_id=40

Scientific Name: Acropora spp.

Common Names: Many common names including staghorn, green slimer, and so on.

Degree of Difficulty: Moderate to difficult, as they need HO lighting, calcium reactors and high water flow. Maintain low levels of nitrate and phosphate as well as constant high levels of calcium from 400 to 450 ppm, magnesium and alkalinity. Feed every week with dissolved marine organics.

pH : 8.2 - 8.4
Temperature: 75° F - 82° F (24° C - 28° C)
Water Hardness: 8° to 12° dH
Calcium: 400 - 450 ppm

Origin: Indo-Pacific, Australia, Indian Ocean, Pacific Ocean

Lighting: High light level such as from T5's and Metal Halides.

Water Movement: High turbulent flow in changing directions.

Frag: The SPS corals are simple to frag. Use a tool for cutting corals or snips for a clean cut.

Note: Keep Acropora Coral in SPS only tanks.

Birdsnest Coral

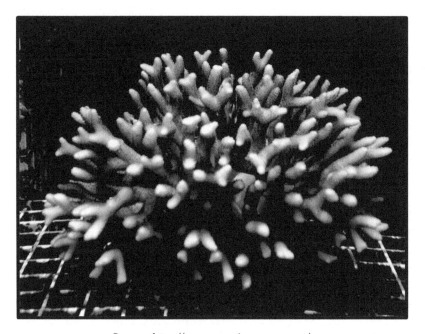

Source: http://www.marinescene.com/

Scientific Name: Seriatopora hystrix

Common Names: Pink Birdsnest Coral

Degree of Difficulty: Moderate to Difficult. Birdsnest coral has stringent water parameter requirements. It can sting and be stung by other corals so it must have space for growing. You do not need to feed Birdsnest coral directly.

pH: 8.2 - 8.4

Temperature: 75° F - 82° F (24° C - 28° C)

Water Hardness: 8° to 12° dH

Calcium: 400 - 450 ppm

Origin: Tonga, the Red Sea, the Indo-Pacific, Fiji.

Lighting: High Lighting Levels with T5's or Metal Halides. Activated carbon is sometimes needed to keep the water clean (polished) and penetrable enough for this coral.

Water Movement: Moderate to high indirect flow is required. Increase the indirect flow to reduce any algae growth.

Frag: Make a clean cut and glue the piece to a frag plug.

Blastomussa Coral

Source: http://www.timothylucas.com/saltyfriends.com

Scientific Name: Blastomussa wellsi

Common Names: Blastomussa Coral, Blasto Pineapple Coral

Degree of Difficulty: Easy to moderate LPS coral. Direct feeding is not needed as they get most nutrients from their zooxanthellae. Not aggressive with other corals and is a good starter coral for beginners.

pH: 8.2 - 8.4
Temperature: 75° F - 82° F (24° C - 28° C)
Water Hardness: 8° to 12° dKH
Calcium: 400 - 450 ppm

Origin: Red Sea and Australia.

Lighting: Moderate lighting levels allow bottom placement with T5's or Metal Halides.

Water Movement: Low to moderate fluctuating varied directional water flow.
Frag: Simply cut a polyp.

Candy Cane Coral

Source: http://successfulreefkeeping.com/about-corals/fragging-future/

Scientific Name: Caulastrea furcata

Common Names: Trumpet coral, torch coral, candy cane coral, bullseye coral

Degree of Difficulty: Easy to moderate LPS coral. Not aggressive so keep it away from aggressive corals with space to grow. Target feed tiny pieces of fresh marine-origining foods when lights are out. Gently place food near feeding tentacles.

pH: 8.1 - 8.4
Temperature: 75° F - 82° F (24° C - 28° C)
Water Hardness: 8° to 12° dH
Calcium: 400 - 450 ppm

Origin: Indo-Pacific, Fiji, Solomon Islands.

Lighting: Moderate lighting with T5's, VHO's or Metal Halides.

Water Movement: Moderate only.

Frag: Easy to frag from low branches and then attach to a frag plug or live rock.

Chalice Coral

Source:
http://www.thecoralzone.com/sps_coral/echinophyllia_chalice_coral.shtml

Scientific Name: Echinophyllia sp., Enchinopora sp., Oxypora sp.

Common Names: Many common names such as chalice, scroll, elephant nose, peacock, plate, antler, palm, hibiscus coral, etc.

Degree of Difficulty: Moderate. Very low levels of nitrate and phosphate. Target feed twice a week with Mysis shrimp and brine shrimp.

pH: 8.2 - 8.4
Temperature: 75° F - 82° F (24° C - 28° C)
Water Hardness: 8° to 12° dH
Calcium: 400 - 450 ppm

Origin: Indo-Pacific to the Red Sea, as well as the northern and eastern coast of Australia.

Lighting: Moderate lighting at the bottom half of the tank.

Water Movement: Moderate and turbulent multi-directional flows.

Frag: Score the underside of the coral to break off a frag. Rinse the frag in tank water in a separate container and use coral glue to attach to a flat frag plug. Rinse again in saltwater. Keep frags at a minimum of one inch.

Frogspawn Coral

Source: http://www.thecoralzone.com/lps_coral/frogspawn_coral.shtml

Scientific Name: Euphyllia divisa

Common Names: Frogspawn coral and Grape Coral.

Degree of Difficulty: Moderate. LPS coral that can be aggressive with long tentacles so give them an abundance of space. Direct feeding periodically once or twice a week of tiny pieces of minced seafood.

pH: 8.1 - 8.4

Temperature: 75° F - 82° F (24° C - 28° C)

Water Hardness: 8° to 12° dH

Calcium: 400 - 420 ppm

Origin: Red Sea, Samoa, Indo-Pacific, Solomon Islands

Lighting: Moderate to High lighting with T5's, VHO's or metal halides.

Water Movement: Moderate flow.

Frag: Cut off some of a branch, leaving as much as possible. Adhere them to a larger piece of live rock with super glue gel or a coral epoxy.

Green Star Polyps Coral

Source: ceruleanlegacy.wordpress.com

Scientific Name: Briareium sp.

Common Names: Green Star Polyps, Starburst Polyps, Purple Mat Polyps, Daisy Polyps

Degree of Difficulty: Easy to moderate. Good beginner coral as standard reef tank water parameters for calcium, alkalinity and pH are all that is needed. Direct feeding is not needed as they get nutrients from photosynthesis. They need space to grow.

pH: 8.2 - 8.4
Temperature: 75° F - 84° F (24° C - 29° C)
Water Hardness: 7° to 11° dH
Calcium: 420 - 500 ppm

Origin: Indo-Pacific, Fiji

Lighting: Moderate to high light levels with T5's and metal halides.

Water Movement: Moderate to high turbulent indirect water flow.

Frag: Use a clean razor blade and slice a piece of the purple mat. Attach this to a frag plug and use a rubber band to fasten it. When the mat has attached remove the rubber band.

Montipora Capricornis Coral

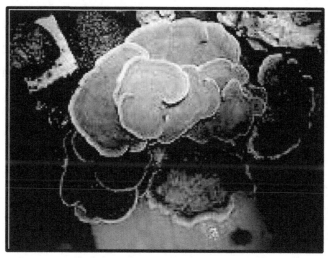

Source: orphek.com

Common Names: Leaf coral, Vase coral, Leaf Plate Coral, Whorled Montipora, Monti Cap

Degree of Difficulty: Moderate to difficult. Non aggressive but fast growth can soon shade other corals. Feeding is not necessary. Popular SPS coral that come in a variety of colors. Needs exceptional water conditions with calcium, alkalinity and pH levels up and nitrates low and phosphates at or as near zero as doable.

pH: 8.1 - 8.4
Temperature: 75° F - 80° F (24° C - 27° C)
Water Hardness: 8° to 12° dH
Calcium: 400 - 420 ppm

Origin: Indo-Pacific, Fiji, Solomon Islands, often found in mid to shallow water levels.

Lighting: Moderate to high lighting levels with T5's, VHO's or metal halides are recommended.

Water Movement: Moderate to high and turbulent flows.

Frag: Easy to frag. Break off a piece and affix to a reef plug with super glue or a saltwater safe bonding agent.

Montipora Digitata

Source: http://www.thecoralzone.com

Scientific Name: Montipora Digitata

Common Names: Montipora digi, monti digi, velvet branch, velvet finger

Degree of Difficulty: Moderate to high. SPS coral often require more specialized equipment like calcium reactors, high output lighting, increased water flow, etc. In general, high water flow, high lighting levels and optimal water conditions are required. They will usually survive without feeding, although some hobbyists do feed them regularly. They need plenty of room to grow.

pH: 8.2 - 8.4
Temperature: 75° F - 82° F (24° C - 28° C)
Water Hardness: 8° to 12° dH
Calcium: 400 - 450 ppm

Origin: Indo-Pacific, Australia, Indian Ocean

Lighting: Moderate to high lighting required with T5's and Metal halide

Water Movement: High turbulent flows with varied directions.

Frag: Easy to frag by breaking a piece off and using superglue to attach to a frag plug. Usually encrusts within a few weeks.

Montipora Spongodes

Source: www.nano-reef.com

Scientific Name: Montipora sp.

Common Names: many including staghorn, green slimer, and so on.

Degree of Difficulty: Moderate. They need moderate to high output lighting and moderate to high water flow with good water quality; Standard reef tank water parameters. Quarantine and dip new coral arrivals. A potassium permanganate dip of 25 to 50 mg/l for about an hour is advised. This is not reef tank safe so treating an entire tank with potassium permanganate solution is not advisable. After the quarantine or dipping, drip acclimate the coral for an hour before tank introduction.

pH: 8.2 - 8.4

Temperature: 75°F - 82°F (24°C - 28°C)

Water Hardness: 8° to 12° dH

Calcium: 400 - 450 ppm

Origin: Grown in captivity.

Lighting: Moderate to high lighting levels. T5's and metal halides.

Water Movement: Moderate to high turbulent flows in varied directions.

Frag: Should be at least 6 inches in size before fragging. Simple break off an inch or so and then super glue to a frag plug.

Pavona Coral

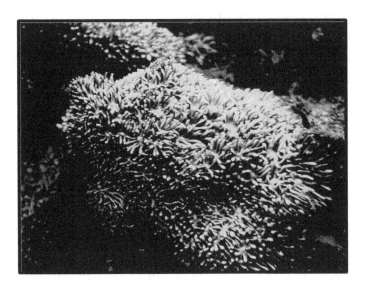

Source: www.dfwmas.org

Scientific Name: Pavona decussata

Common Names: Cactus coral, Cabbage coral

Degree of Difficulty: Moderate to high. Considered an SPS coral. They will do well in moderate to high lighting with moderate to high turbulent water flows. This coral needs excellent water conditions and room to grow.

Monitor nitrate and phosphate levels as these will prohibit growth. Optionally target feed, but do not allow food waste to accumulate in your tank.

pH: 8.2 - 8.4

Temperature: 75° F - 82° F (24° C - 28° C)

Water Hardness: 8° to 12° dH

Calcium: 400 - 450 ppm

Origin: Indo-Pacific, Australia, Indian Ocean, along the middle to upper East coast of Africa

Lighting: Moderate to high light levels. Metal halides, T5-HO and high output LEDs.

Water Movement: Turbulent flows in multiple directions and varied patterns.

Frag: Break a piece off and use super glue to adhere to a frag plug.

Pulsing Xenia

Source: www.garf.org

Scientific Name: Xenia sp.

Common Names: Pulsing Xenia, Pulse Coral, Hand Coral

Degree of Difficulty: Moderate to challenging. These coral require a minimum 30-gallon or 114-liter tank. Do not keep with coral nibblers, such as crab and starfish. No additional feeding is usually necessary. They are mobile and can pull themselves to different locations.

pH: 8.2 - 8.5
Temperature: 75° F - 80° F (25°C - 27° C)
Specific Gravity: 1.023 - 1.025

Carbonate Hardness (dKH) : 8 - 12°
Calcium Levels: 300 - 420 mg/L

Origin: Reefs

Lighting: High Output (HO), VHO or metal halides. Lighting is required for photosynthesis, though they also eat dissolved nutrients.

Water movement: The polyps will pulse or open and close and no one knows exactly why although there are a lot of theories. Slow flow is the best water movement for the Pulsing Xenia.

Warning: Some xenia corals release chemicals that can be a danger to stony corals.

Ricordea florida

Source: http://momenticoncepts.com/newageaquatics/corals/mushrooms/36-
atomic-green-orange-sherbet-ricordia

Scientific Name: Ricordea florida

Common Names: False Coral, Mushroom coral,
Corallimorph

Degree of Difficulty: Easy with common lighting and
water parameters although they should be restricted from
contact with other coral.

pH: 8.1 - 8.4
Temperature: 75° F - 82° F (24° C - 28° C)
Water Hardness: 8° to 12° dH
Calcium: 400 - 420 ppm

Origin: Caribbean

Lighting: Moderate to high lighting levels with T5's, VHO's or metal halides. Slow acclimation to light intensity over several weeks is recommended.

Water Movement: Moderate with periodic turbulent flows.

Frag: Frag with a clean razor blade by cutting in half and attaching to live rock rubble.

Zoanthids

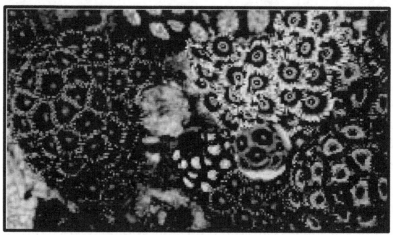

Source: http://saltwaterplus.wordpress.com/2013/03/30/coral-corner-zoanthids/

Degree of Difficulty: Easy to moderate makes this coral great for beginners. They get most nutrients from tank lighting and filter feeding on bacteria.

pH: 8.2 - 8.4

Temperature: 75° F - 80° F (24° C - 27° C)

Alkalinity: 8° to 10° dKH

Calcium: 400 - 420 ppm

Origin: Many places.

Lighting: They need moderate to bright light.

Water Movement: Fair to high and turbulent flows.

Frag: Easy to frag with live rock rubble.

Warning: There are species of zoanthids that are toxic to humans. Always wear gloves when working with them or being exposed to tank water. Wash thoroughly when you are done.

7. Plants

Freshwater aquarium plants are appreciated by any fish inhabitants. Place them according to the design elements discussed earlier. Aquascaping with live freshwater aquarium plants requires additional effort, but can open a new world to your creative juices. Many plants can be trimmed for the desired shape.

To increase the odds of your success choose hardy species to gain the experience of placing and caring for freshwater aquarium plants. There are basically a few common types of freshwater aquarium plants:

- Floating plants such as Fairy Moss and Riccia which can provide shelter for young fish.
- Rhizomes have thick stems with leaves at the top. They root in the substrate and grow across the substrate surface.
- The rosette style plant grows fast and can quickly cover substrate.
- A stem plant roots in the substrate and is available in a variety of colors and of types.
- Java Moss is great for freshwater aquariums that can grow in a range of water parameters and pH with low light requirements.
- Water wisteria is great for beginners. This plant grows fast and helps control algae by eradicating nitrates from the water.

- Anubias nana is hearty plant that usually grows in most all water parameters that can flower and grows out of the water as well.
- Amazon Sword is an easy species to grow and also helps maintain algae.

Growing Healthy Plants

Photosynthesis is how plants convert hydrogen, oxygen and carbon molecules into the basic sugars which create energy and food for plants. Chlorophyll is a blend of two pigments, chlorophyll and chlorophyll B, which enable the process of photosynthesis to occur. Additional aquarium plant pigments are present; such as the orange pigment carotene or the yellow pigment xanthophylls, although these pigments are not part of the photosynthesis process.

When plants are not getting adequate light, an unhealthy yellow color appears because there is a decrease in the green pigment of chlorophyll. This can frequently be the result of an iron deficiency.

Exposing chlorophyll to light results in photosynthesis. As we learned in the previous chapter on lighting, photosynthesis and respiration are the two processes that occur in plants needed for healthy plants to break down nutrients and grow. These processes occur during the phases of the cycle of light and dark.

When photosynthesis has taken place, during respiration plants will receive oxygen as well as create heat energy and carbon dioxide. During the dark period, they respire CO_2 in the aquarium and higher concentrations of CO_2 and light will boost the action of chlorophyll.

Your aquascape must mimic the amount of light and dark naturally required by the plants. Depending on where a specific plant species evolved, a specific light or darkness period will be optimal. Sometimes, depending on the amount of plants and fish, your aquascape might need carbon dioxide supplementation. You can use a soda bottle filled with yeast, warm water, and sugar. Connect that to an air stone in the tank or a pressurized CO_2 tank that instills a predetermined quantity of carbon dioxide.

Research the needs of any plants you choose. If you select different species, make sure they have compatible requirements. In a biotope aquarium, the plants share the same geographical location and environment so this is easier. Live aquarium plants help aeration, filtration, as well as food and algae control for healthier inhabitants.

There are aquarium-safe fertilizers that come in liquid or tablet form. Some substrates contain laterite which also provides nutrients.

8. Set Up, Maintenance and Testing

Setting up and maintaining an aquascape can be intimidating for beginners. While the process is complex, knowledge will instill confidence and increase your chances of success.

Sump Setup

A sump is a separate tank that gets water from a gravity overflow in your aquarium. Water rises over the top of the overflow and into a pipe to the sump. A return pump sends the water back to the tank. The aquarium sump can hide unsightly equipment, increase the total water volume, and make changing water easier. Saltwater supplements can be put into the sump to dissolve before going into your tank.

Refugium Setup

The refugium is a separate tank used to extract nitrates, phosphates, carbon dioxide and other nutrients from the water by "harvesting" the macro algae. Macro algae also support many advantageous life forms like amphipods and copepods that can feed fish and corals. Refugiums usually require a light source and a deep sand bed.

Filters

There are hobbyists who use mechanical filters, such as a power filter or canister filter, and those who use only protein skimmers. The mechanical filters are optional and can also only be used at certain times such as when there is algae growth.

A protein skimmer works well to remove the majority of most organics, so a power filter is not always needed. Mechanical filters require regular cleaning every few days to prevent nitrate issues.

Protein Skimmer

A protein skimmer can be used as a standalone, hang on the side of the tank, or used in a sump. Protein skimmers are not always required for a saltwater reef tank.

Performing regular water changes can be done in place of using a protein skimmer for aquariums, with few inhabitants if you are experienced.

When curing live rock and using a protein skimmer, keep an eye on the collection cup. This might fill up quickly in the beginning.

Starting Your System

Once you have everything in place, turn your system on and let it run for a few days and up to a week. Test the water daily for any ammonia or nitrites. When there are none but you can perceive small amounts of nitrates, your water is ready for inhabitants. Live rock can be so good at denitrification that your water might not get a nitrate reading.

Quarantine Period

Add inhabitants to your aquarium slowly and be certain to use a quarantine tank. While this adds a step to the process this is cheap insurance. Since you likely pay for fish and coral, this will help ensure your inhabitants survive as well as protect your investment.

All fish and corals should remain in a quarantine tank for several weeks to be observed for signs of infection such as saltwater fish disease. Be prepared to treat them immediately. A quarantine tank gives fish a chance to distress from transport and an opportunity for you to observe and inspect them.

Since corals can also transmit diseases, you would be wise to dip them in Lugol's Solution (concentrated iodine) for 10 - 15 minutes prior to placing them in a quarantine tank. You can also get pest dips to prevent things like montipora eating nudibranchs, acropora, or flatworms.

Activated Carbon

Carbon helps remove dissolved nutrients and smells as well as clean aquarium water. Activated carbon must be replaced regularly; how often depends on your tank situation.

Activated carbon comes in a variety of grades. Some are better at leeching compounds and others release phosphates into the water. A reef tank can benefit from activated carbon since they also help solve algae issues. Be careful when changing a large amount of activated carbon in your tank. This can shock your corals. Replace one-third to one-half at a time.

Tank Set Up

Selecting a location for your aquarium involves several considerations from light to weight. A location that gets direct sunlight could be good or bad, depending on your inhabitants. Generally direct sunlight is not good as this can heat up your tank water and disrupt any special light cycles.

Water in aquariums weighs from 8 to 12 pounds per gallon. A 100-gallon tank could weigh over 1,000 pounds so you need to know the capability of the floor and structure where you will place the tank. If you have any questions, consult an engineer or other professional.

Also consider the consequences of a leak and what damage the total amount of water in your tank could do. If you live on an upper floor of an apartment, for instance, other people could be affected. Check with your insurance agent to see what you are covered for.

Consider how much room you need around the tank for maintenance and comfortable viewing. Placing your tank where maintenance is difficult can make you regret your hobby and even neglect your tank.

Reef Tank Setup Equipment Needed:

- Aquarium
- Lights
- Light Timer
- Salt Mix
- Sand
- Live Rock
- Protein Skimmer
- Power Filter (optional)
- Algae Scraper
- Sump and/or Refugium (optional)
- Quarantine Tank
- Power heads (multiple)
- Food
- Thermometer
- Heater
- Test Kits (chlorine, pH, ammonia, nitrite, nitrate, phosphate, calcium, alkalinity, iodine)

- Reverse Osmosis filter (optional)
- Hydrometer or refractometer
- 2 Clean Five Gallon Buckets
- Fish, Corals and other Invertebrates
- Macro Algae such as chaetomorpha or gracilaria for use in the refugium

Test for Leaks

Make sure your aquarium is level and fill your tank at the chosen location while watching for leaks. If you use any type of hose to fill your tank do not use high pressure and be careful not to tap the glass with a metal hose end or attachment. Aquarium glass can break easier than most people assume.

Make sure to use de-chlorinated tap water or reverse osmosis water. For salt water set-ups, add the pre-measured salt mix when the tank is about two-thirds full.

Turn on power heads to keep the water flowing. After several hours, test the specific gravity with a hydrometer. This should be in the range of 1.023 - 1.025.

If the specific gravity is too high, you can remove some of the tank water and add freshwater only. If the specific gravity is too low then add more salt mix.

The Nitrogen Cycle Source

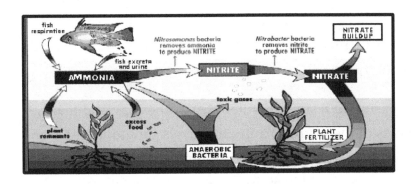

beilerbiology.blogspot.com/p/nitrogen-cycle.html

The nitrogen cycle is a sequence of events that anatomizes fish waste turning it into nitrogen. A new aquarium will form different types of bacteria and needs to be tested throughout the first cycle. The cycle:

1. Ammonia is produced from fish waste, live rock or discarded food. The waste will break down into harmless ammonium or harmful ammonia.

2. Aerobic bacteria form and break ammonia into nitrites (NO2) that are non-toxic in salt water.

3. As more bacteria grow, they turn harmless nitrites into nitrates (NO3) which are not as damaging as the ammonia.

4. Anaerobic bacteria that dwell in live rock and sand bed substrate turn the nitrates into safe nitrogen gas.

Starting the nitrogen cycle can be done with small fish, live rock or small amounts of food. Live rock is often enough for saltwater aquariums. You will see ammonia levels increase in two or three days. If not, you can add a bit of food.

You should test your water every other day and make notes of the results. Ammonia levels should increase and then fall. When ammonia is falling, nitrite ought to rise. Then nitrite will increase, peak, and then fall. When the ammonia and nitrite have followed this pattern and then test zero or the nitrate is less than 20 ppm, the cycle has occurred and the water is ready for inhabitants.

There are "bacteria starters" that speed up the nitrogen cycle. Some aquariums cycle within only two weeks and others can need up to two months. There are many factors involved. Using water from an established aquarium does not speed up the process.

Create a Log

Recording test data can be very beneficial in determining what is happening in your aquarium and alert you to corrections you might need to make. Use a notebook or computer to keep notes on tank parameters and test results each time you test. A spreadsheet with column labels for each test such as ammonia, nitrite, nitrate, pH, etc. and dates in the column will work well. Once you collect several weeks of data you can create graphs for more information on trends. Some hobbyists also photograph their tanks each week to see development.

Schedule Maintenance

Create a list of daily and weekly tasks including feeding and testing.

For example:

- You will want to scrape the glass to remove diatom algae growth. You can use an aquarium vacuum over the substrate or sand to remove any algae.
- Empty and scrub the protein skimmer collection cup.
- Add filtered water to replace any evaporation loss.
- Check the levels of nitrate, pH, alkalinity, calcium, phosphate and silicate. Replenish calcium and maintain alkalinity levels for coral growth. A calcium reactor can help maintain the calcium level automatically.
- Clean power heads and skimmers.

Testing

Testing your aquarium is vital for keeping the inhabitants healthy. A few recommended test kits are for ammonia, nitrite, nitrate, phosphate, pH (pH meter), iodine, calcium, alkalinity and a hydrometer. Test your water regularly and record the results.

There are numerous aquarium test kits including:

- Ammonia
- Nitrite
- Nitrate
- Salinity/Specific Gravity
- pH
- Carbonate Water Hardness
- Alkalinity
- Chlorine and Chloramine
- Copper
- Phosphate
- Dissolved Oxygen
- Iron and Carbon Dioxide

Master test kits are available that suffice for most tanks. A master test kit for fresh water tanks commonly includes ammonia, nitrite, nitrate and pH testing. A saltwater master kit includes tests for ammonia, nitrite, nitrate, pH and alkalinity. Some plant, coral, and saltwater tanks might need other test kits for copper, phosphate, dissolved oxygen, and more.

Some test kits are dip strips and others are liquid drop testers. Usually you use something such as a test tube containing a sample of your tank water and dip a test strip in and then compare the color results against the kit information or color card. The liquid drop test requires you place drops in a test tube with your tank water and then compare the color of the water with a test card.

General recommended saltwater reef tank water parameters:

- Specific Gravity 1.023 - 1.025
- Temperature 75 F to 80 F (24° C - 27° C)
- Calcium 400 - 450 ppm
- Alkalinity - 2.1 to 2.5 meq/L
- Magnesium - 1200 - 1400 ppm
- Ammonia, Nitrite, Nitrates and Phosphate - 0 ppm
- Iodine - 0.06 meq/L

Alkalinity Test

An alkalinity test establishes the buffering capacity or ability of a tank to maintain pH level. A desirable test result for saltwater is 7 to 12 dkH.

Ammonia Test

Produced by waste and discarded food, ammonia is the number one reason for tropical fish fatalities. This should test at a zero level.

Calcium Test

Corals devour more calcium from the water as they develop and will need to be replenished. Calcium measuring is vital when adding calcium in reef aquascapes. Saltwater corals require calcium and a test kit will help you to verify how much you need and how often.

Chloramine Test

Chloramine is made from chlorine and ammonia. This is a disinfectant and you need to eliminate this from your environment just as you do chlorine from tap water - or this can kill your fish.

Chlorine Test

Chlorine is in most tap water and you need to make sure there is no chlorine in your aquarium prior to introducing any fish or other life.

Copper Test

Copper is a heavy metal that can be harmful as well as fatal to your fish and invertebrates. Copper can be introduced into your tank if your water supply has older pipes made of copper or through the use of any medications that contain copper.

Iodine Test

Saltwater with corals or invertebrates requiring iodine needs iodine-testing to determine doses. Iodine depletes through consumption and is reduced by protein skimmers.

Magnesium Test

Saltwater naturally has 1200 to 1400 ppm (parts per million) of magnesium. You want to maintain this level.

Nitrate Test

As discussed in the section on the Nitrogen cycle, nitrites are transformed to *nitrates* in the nitrogen cycle. Nitrates can be toxic and, although not as dangerous to your fish as ammonia or nitrites, they do stress them at higher levels.

Nitrite Test

Nitrite and ammonia are toxic to your fish, so you want a nitrite test to be zero. A complete water change is needed to reduce nitrite levels.

pH Test

The pH scale ranges from zero to fourteen and measures the acidity or alkalinity of water. Zero is the most acidic, seven is neutral and fourteen the most alkaline. Because different fish species need diverse pH levels, keeping inhabitants in your tank that require similar pH levels is advisable.

Phosphate Test

Phosphate comes from tap water, dead plants and discarded fish food. High phosphate levels can result in algae outbreaks and retard coral growth. You can purchase a Phosphate Test Kit.

Salinity Test

A salinity test measures the dissolved salts in water. A hydrometer or refracto-meter is utilized to conduct this test.

Specific Gravity Test

The specific gravity test measures the density of salts in saltwater in contrast to freshwater by comparison of weight.

Water Hardness Test

Water hardness level relates to the minerals dissolved in the water. Hard water contains multiple, while soft water has few. The chief concern is very soft water which can dramatically affect the pH level. Salt water's carbonate hardness is a good indication of the stability of the water's pH level.

Appendix

http://www.adana.co.jp/en/

http://www.plantedaquariumscentral.com/Guide_to_Aqu
ascaping

Plant Index

http://www.aquascapingworld.com/plantpedia/list_view
_plant.php?where=&search_type=simple&sort=scientific_
name&search=View%20Complete%20Index&show=40

U.S. State Restricted Plants
http://www.plantedaquariumscentral.com/State_restricte
d_Plants.html

Glossary

Aerobic: Plants and other organisms that require oxygen.

Acclimate: Acclimation is the procedure of introducing fish or other animals into a new environment or aquarium water.

Acidic: In reference to the pH scale. Water with a pH balance of less than 7 is considered acidic. Water measuring over pH 7 is basic or alkaline and 7 the neutral level.

Actinic Light: Blue wave length lighting. This light can penetrate deeper than other wave lengths, highlight colors in corals and aid coralline algae growth.

Activated Carbon: a form of carbon that removes dissolved nutrients and smells; it helps clean the aquarium water.

Air Pump: Aquarium air pump that pumps air into aquarium tubing.

Air Stone: Stones made from sand or lime wood for air diffusing.

Aeration: Increasing tank air using air stones or power heads pointed at the water surface.

Ahermatypic: corals that do not host symbiotic zooxanthellae and are sometimes referred to as the "non reef building" corals.

Algae : Algae can appear on most any surface in an aquarium as brown diatoms, blue-green algae, green algae and red algae. There are unwanted and desired algae (coralline algae in saltwater aquariums.) Algae require carbon dioxide, phosphates, nitrates and iron to grow. Restricting amounts of these nutrients helps control unwanted algae.

Algaecide: This chemical kills algae although can be dangerous to other aquarium inhabitants.

Algae Turf Scrubber: turf scrubber or algal scrubber is a filtration method where aquarium water is moved into a separate tank as a sump, for example, where the water is cleaned.

Alkaline: relates to the pH scale when the pH is over 7.

Ammonia: ammonia derives from discarded fish foods, wastes and other biological processes in the aquarium. Biological filtration is required to remove ammonia because this is toxic, and likely the number one killer of aquarium fish.

Anaerobic: condition where there is no oxygen. It can also describe an organism that does not require oxygen.

Anoxic: low oxygen levels in aquarium water.

Aragonite: a form of calcium carbonate used to increase or preserve high pH and alkalinity levels.

Bacteria: microscopic organisms in aquariums. Some of these are harmful, but the majority of them are beneficial and needed for the nitrogen cycle.

Bare Bottom: an aquarium without substrate.

Bio-load: the computed total of the biological burden on the biological filter in an aquarium.

Bio-wheel: round biological filtration product that spins using water motion to mix air needed for good bacteria to colonize.

Biological Filtration: aquarium filter system that encourages or supports growing good bacteria.

Brackish Tank: Small amounts of dissolved salts in the water (less than salt water.)

Buffer: powder or chemical utilized to alter the alkalinity level of tank water so the water can defy transformations in the aquarium pH level. Saltwater aquariums can require buffer agents that are commonly carbonate and bicarbonate.

Calcium: mineral required by corals, clams and some algae. The calcium level ranges between 380 - 450 mg/L in natural salt water.

Calcium Carbonate: $CaCO_3$. This element is often a needed supplement for salt water tanks as they are needed by coral to grow.

Canister Filter: external filter that pulls water from the aquarium and pumps it through an assortment of filters and then back into the tank. They can have multiple filters, such as an activated carbon filter and a zeolite filter.

Chemical Filter: filter such as activated carbon that removes dissolved nutrients from the aquarium.

Chloramine: NH_2CL is in some tap water and is harmful to fish so the water must be neutralized before fish are introduced.

Chiller: a device to cool tank water.

Chlorine: chlorine is used in tap water and is toxic to fish. Always use water conditioners that eradicate chlorine and chloramines.

CO2: carbon dioxide, the byproduct of fish respiration.

CO2 System: a carbon dioxide system that injects carbon dioxide into freshwater aquariums.

Commensalism: a type of symbiosis where one organism benefits from the relationship but the other organism is impervious.

Coralline Algae: plant that grows with light and calcium to grow in colors on live rock and tank walls.

Crustacean: hard exoskeleton invertebrates such as lobsters, crabs and shrimps.

Cyanobacteria: unwanted bacteria commonly called "Red Slime Algae." Possibly the result of low water flows, high amounts of dissolved nutrients, and even a wrong spectrum of lighting.

Dechlorinator: water additive to remove chlorine and chloramine from tap water.

Deionization: the process of removing ions from water.

Denitrification: process when nitrates are transformed into nontoxic nitrogen gas that dissipates at water surface.

Diatomaceous Earth: soft rock from fossilized diatom algae crushed into powder for diatom filters.

Diatom Filter: mechanical filter that pumps tank water through packed diatomaceous earth substance to clean or polish the water. Because they block easily they are used only used sporadically.

Dissolved Oxygen: oxygen dissolved in tank water available for inhabitants and measured as a saturation level or in PPM.

Distilled Water: boiling where the steam is collected to remove solids, salts and organics.

Diurnal: animal, plant or fish that is lively during the daytime.

DOC: Dissolved Organic Carbon or Dissolved Organic Compounds.

Dolomite: carbonate rock made up of calcium magnesium carbonate.

Endemic: fish or animal that is native to a specific location.

Frag: short for coral fragment.

Full Spectrum Light: light such as sunlight that exhibits the full spectrum of visible light.

GH: General Hardness is a measurement for the sum of dissolve minerals in a tank.

GPH: Gallons Per Hour.

Green Water: usually caused by nutrients that are not dissolved, causing algae. It does not usually hurt fish.

Hard Water: water that is full of numerous minerals. Reverse Osmosis filters are used to soften hard water.

Herbivore: fish that eat mostly plants, algae, and/or plant matter.

HO Light: HO lamps usually produce 20 to 60 watts. T5 lights are HO lights.

Hydrometer: device that measures specific gravity of tank water used with brackish and saltwater aquariums.

Invertebrate: animals without a backbone such as shrimp, crab, coral, snails and more.

Iodine: a saltwater aquarium supplement. Always test before dosing with iodine. Natural sea water iodine concentration equals: 0.03 - 0.06 mg/L (ppm).

Kelvin: scale for thermodynamic temperature used for referencing the color of fluorescent lighting. A candle flame equals about 1800° and daylight equals about 6500°.

LED: Light Emitting Diode. LED lights are cooler, use less energy and last longer than other types of lighting.

LPH: Liters Per Hour.

Light Meter: measures light intensity.

Limewood Diffuser: limewood diffuser creates tiny air bubbles. It is sometimes placed in protein skimmers or used with under gravel filters.

Live Rock: rubble that has broken off the coral reef. Quality live rock is particularly porous and supports colonizing bacteria needed in the nitrogen cycle.

Live Sand: sand populated with beneficial bacteria, invertebrates and other organisms.

Lumens: total production of a light source.

Lux: measurement of the intensity of light.

Lux Meter: device that measures lux, or light intensity. You can use a lux meter to find the best locations for coral in the tank.

Magnesium: element Mg, is the third most plentiful element in natural sea water. A magnesium test kit will tell you if you have enough in your water. Low levels can affect calcium and alkalinity levels.

Mechanical Filter: aquarium filter that removes larger particles from tank water.

Metal Halide : high intensity light for growing coral in saltwater reef tanks and plants in freshwater tanks. Because of the heat they produce an aquarium chiller may be needed to maintain water temperature.

mg/L: milligrams per liter or comparable to PPM.

Mutualism: a form of symbiosis where two organisms get some advantage from their involvement with one other.

Nanometer: (nm) equal to one billionth of a meter and used to reference the wavelength of light in aquarium lighting. Varying light wavelengths create different colors. The human eye can only see light from 380 nm (violet) to 780 nm (red).

Nitrate: NO3, occurs at the end of the aquarium nitrogen cycle. Harmful to fish in higher concentrations.

Nitrite: NO2, part of the aquarium nitrogen cycle where ammonia is converted to nitrites and nitrites are transformed into nitrates.

Nitrogen Cycle: the aquarium nitrogen cycle is the conversion of ammonia to nitrite and then nitrites to nitrates by favorable bacteria.

Nocturnal: animals or fish that sleep in the day and are active at night or in the dark.

Omnivore: animal or fish that eats meat and plants.

Overflow Box: hangs on the back of the tank to drain water from the tank into a sump.

Ozone: O3, an unstable gas that is every now and then utilized to augment dissolved oxygen content in aquarium water.

Parasitism: form of symbiosis where an organism benefits from the relationship and the other organism is harmed.

pH: water measurement on a logarithmic scale to determine an acidic, neutral or alkaline state.

Phosphate: PO4, phosphorous and oxygen, a prime constituent for algae.

Power Compact Light: U-shaped fluorescent light, 9 watts through 96 watts, that generates more light than standard fluorescent tubes. They do generate heat so a fan might be helpful.

Power Filter: a mechanical filtration, biological filtration and chemical filtration system. Water is pumped through a replaceable filter with activated carbon and some have a course media where water exits for bacterial colonizing.

Powerhead: creates water movement inside the aquarium.

PPM: Parts Per Million equivalent to mg/L.

Protein Skimmer: a saltwater aquarium filtration mechanism that takes out dissolved organics from the water by means of a procedure known as foam fractionation.

Refractometer: used to measure the salinity of water.

Reverse Osmosis: water filtration system where water is pumped through a semi-permeable membrane to separate "bad" atoms from good. Reverse osmosis water is as much as 90% more pure than tap water.

Salinity: measurement of the total amount of dissolved salts in saltwater.

Sessile: organisms (invertebrates) that do not freely move around the tank and attach to the substrate, live rock or other surface.

Substrate: bottom of the aquarium that can be gravel, sand or mud.

Sump: aquarium connected to the main tank for increasing the total amount of volume in the system.

Symbiosis: when two different types of organisms live in close association. Categories of symbiosis include: mutualism, commensalism, parasitism, amensalism, neutralism and competition.

T5 HO: a High Output fluorescent light 5/8 inch in diameter.

TDS: Total Dissolved Solids. Measure with a TDS meter to track the performance of reverse osmosis.

Target Feeding: process for filter feeders (corals) where food is delivered directly to the coral.

Timer: electrical device for turning devices on and off.

Trickle Filter: aquarium filter that integrates a type of wet-dry filtration where aquarium water is dripped over plastic bio-balls that are in part exposed to air.

Turn Over: the amount of water flowing through a filter or the total amount of water movement in the tank. Often expressed in GPH (Gallons Per Hour.)

Under Gravel Filter: filter placed under the substrate with rising corner tubes.

Venturi Valve: used in protein skimmers to draw in air and mix with water to create micro-bubbles.

VHO: Very High Output fluorescent aquarium lighting commonly ranging from 75-160 watts.

Water Parameters: measurement of various levels of ammonia, nitrite, pH, nitrate, phosphate, calcium, magnesium, alkalinity, and so on in an aquarium as well as the temperature.

Water Pump: pump that moves aquarium water for filtering or to increase the water movement in the tank.

Wave Maker: device that simulates waves in the aquarium.

Wet-Dry Filter: filter that incorporates dry air in the filtration process to increase biological filtration.

Yellow Water: caused by large amounts of DOC or Dissolved Organic Carbons.

Zeolite: mineral used in chemical filtration of aquariums to remove ammonia from the tank water.

Bibliography

- Borneman, Eric (2004). *Aquarium Corals, Selection Husbandry and Natural History.* T.F.H. Publications

- Calfo, Anthony (2007), *Second Edition, Book of Coral Propagation.* Reading Trees Publications.

- Sprung, Julian (1999), *Corals: A Quick Reference Guide.* Ricordea Publishing.

Index

About the Author

Moe Martin is a photographer who is also interested in many animals - including aquarium-dwellers. He decided to marry his two interests when he discovered Aquascaping. This idea of art and animal life intertwined has had him hooked on the aesthetic nature of the hobby.

Moe is also the lover of all animals, and has more than he can count of the 4-legged variety, all the way down to fish. He lives on a small acreage with his two children and hopes they carry on educating others on the fascinating animals discovered along the way.

Made in the USA
Las Vegas, NV
07 December 2020

12244518R00075